minedition
verlegt in der Michael Neugebauer Edition GmbH, Kiel

Gesetzt wurde in der Neugebauer Rustica and Neugebauer Kursiv entworfen von
Friedrich Neugebauer; digitalisiert von Jovica Veljovic.
Lithografie: Fotoreproduzioni Grafiche, Verona
Koproduktion mit Michael Neugebauer Publishing Ltd. Hong Kong

ISBN 3-86566-030-4
Bibliografische Information der Deutschen Bibliothek
Die Deutsche Bibliothek verzeichnet diese Publikation in der Deutschen Nationalbibliografie;
detaillierte bibliografische Daten sind im Internet über http://dnb.ddb.de abrufbar.

Mehr Information über unsere Bücher finden Sie unter:
www.minedition.com

THE NIGHT BEFORE CHRISTMAS
DIE NACHT VOR WEIHNACHTEN

CLEMENT CLARKE MOORE

MIT BILDERN VON LISBETH ZWERGER

Übersetzung von Erich Kästner

MINEDITION

'Twas the night before Christmas, when all through the house
Not a creature was stirring, not even a mouse;
The stockings were hung by the chimney with care,
In hopes that Saint Nicholas soon would be there.

In der Nacht vor dem Christfest, da regte im Haus
sich niemand und nichts, nicht mal eine Maus.
Die Strümpfe, die hingen paarweis am Kamin
und warteten drauf, daß Sankt Niklas erschien.

The children were nestled all snug in their beds,
While visions of sugar-plums danced in their heads;
And Mamma in her kerchief, and I in my cap,
Had just settled down for a long winter's nap,

Die Kinder lagen gekuschelt im Bett
und träumten vom Apfel- und Nüsseballett.
Die Mutter schlief tief, und auch ich schlief brav,
wie die Murmeltiere im Winterschlaf,

When out on the lawn there rose such a clatter,
I sprang from the bed to see what was the matter.
Away to the window I flew like a flash,
Tore open the shutters and threw up the sash.

als draußen vorm Hause ein Lärm losbrach,
daß ich aufsprang und dachte: Siehst rasch einmal nach!
Ich rannte zum Fenster, und fast noch im Lauf
stieß ich die knarrenden Läden auf.

The moon on the breast of the new-fallen snow
Gave a luster of mid-day to objects below,
When, what to my wondering eyes should appear,
But a miniature sleigh, and eight tiny reindeer,

Es hatte geschneit, und der Mondschein lag
so silbern auf allem, als sei's heller Tag.
Acht winzige Rentierchen kamen gerannt,
vor einem ganz, ganz kleinen Schlitten gespannt!

With a little old driver, so lively and quick,
I knew in a moment it must be St. Nick.
More rapid than eagles his coursers they came,
And he whistled, and shouted, and called them by name –

Auf dem Bock saß ein Kutscher, so alt und so klein,
dass ich wusste, das kann nur der Nikolaus sein!
Die Rentiere kamen daher wie der Wind,
und der Alte, der pfiff, und er rief:" Geschwind!

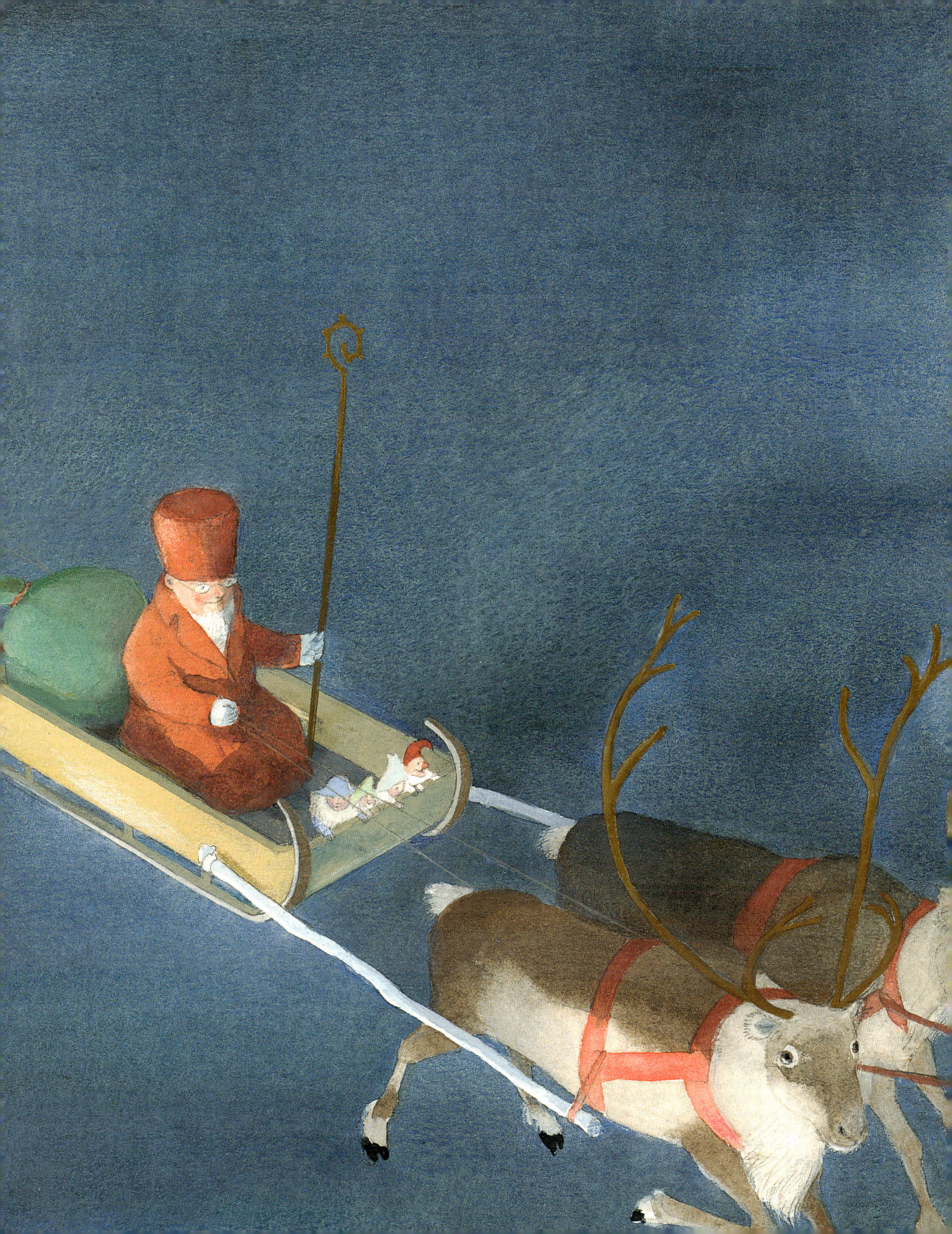

"Now, Dasher, now, Dancer! Now, Prancer and Vixen!
On, Comet! On, Cupid! On, Donder and Blitzen!
To the top of the porch, to the top of the wall,
Now, dash away, dash away, dash away all!"

Renn, Renner! Tanz, Tänzer! Flieg, fliegende Hitz'!
Hui, Sternschnupp'! Hui, Donner und Blitz!
Die Veranda hinauf, und die Hauswand hinan!
Immer fort mit euch! Fort mit euch! Hui, mein Gespann!"

As dry leaves that before the wild hurricane fly,
When they meet with an obstacle, mount to the sky,
So up to the house-top the coursers they flew;
With the sleigh full of toys, – and St. Nicholas too.

Wie das Laub, das der Herbststurm die Straßen lang fegt
und, steht was im Weg, in den Himmel hoch trägt,
so trug es den Schlitten auf unser Haus
samt dem Spielzeug und samt dem Sankt Nikolaus!

And then in a twinkling, I heard on the roof
The prancing and pawing of each little hoof.
As I drew in my head, and was turning around,
Down the chimney St. Nicholas came with a bound.

Kaum war das geschehen, vernahm ich schon schwach
das Stampfen der zierlichen Hufe vom Dach.
Dann wollt' ich die Fensterläden zuzieh'n,
da plumpste der Nikolaus in den Kamin!

He was dressed all in fur, from his head to his foot,
And his clothes were all tarnished with ashes and soot;
A bundle of toys he had flung on his back,
And he looked like a peddler just opening his pack.

Sein Rock war aus Pelzwerk, vom Kopf bis zum Fuß.
Jetzt klebte er freilich voll Asche und Ruß.
Sein Bündel trug Nikolaus huckepack,
so wie die Hausierer bei uns im Sack.

His eyes – how they twinkled! His dimples how merry!
His cheeks were like roses, his nose like a cherry!
His droll little mouth was drawn up like a bow,
And the beard on his chin was as white as the snow.
The stump of the pipe he held tight in his teeth,
And the smoke, it encircled his head like a wreath.
He had a broad face and a little round belly,
That shook when he laughed like a bowlful of jelly.
He was chubby and plump, a right jolly old elf,
And I laughed when I saw him, in spite of myself.
A wink of his eye and a twist of his head,
Soon gave me to know I had nothing to dread.

Zwei Grübchen, wie lustig! Wie blitzte sein Blick!
Die Bäckchen zartrosa, die Nas' rot und dick!
Der Bart war schneeweiß, und der drollige Mund
sah aus wie gemalt, so klein und halbrund.
Im Munde, da qualmte ein Pfeifenkopf,
und der Rauch, der umwand
wie ein Kranz seinen Schopf.

Ich lachte hell, wie er so vor mir stand,
ein rundlicher Zwerg aus dem Elfenland.
Er schaute mich an und schnitt ein Gesicht,
als wollte er sagen: „Nun, fürchte dich nicht!"

He spoke not a word, but went straight to his work,
And filled all the stockings, then turned with a jerk,
And laying his finger aside of his nose,
And giving a nod, up the chimney he rose.

Das Spielzeug stopfte er, eifrig und stumm,
in die Strümpfe, war fertig, drehte sich um,
hob den Finger zur Nase, nickte mir zu,
kroch in den Kamin und war fort im Nu!

He sprang to his sleigh, to his team gave a whistle,
And away they all flew like the down of a thistle.
But I heard him exclaim, 'ere he drove out of sight,
"Merry Christmas to All,
and to All a Good Night."

In den Schlitten sprang er und pfiff dem Gespann,
da flogen sie schon über Tal und Tann.
Doch ich hört' ihn noch rufen, von fern klang es sacht:
„Frohe Weihnachten allen,
und allen gut' Nacht!"